Acknowledgement

This book is written with the intent to educate and entertain. It neither advocates nor denounces sports gambling. Most books on this subject tend to be self-glossing, commercial or overly complicated. I wanted a book that is for everyone, from the novice who wants to learn, to the pro who wants to refresh, and the addicted who wants to quit. The sports gambling world is growing and constantly evolving. People should be as aware and informed as they can be. The chapters of **Terms and Definitions** and **Things You Must Know** are especially important. This book took a long time and a lot of work to complete. Along the way, I have received both support and criticism, and I have some acknowledgements and comments to make.

Thanks to my son Jeremy and my ex-wife Trisha for believing in me.

Thanks to Ed Zaloom for helping to turn on an athletic light for me.

Thanks to my dad, the most intelligent man I ever knew, I miss you.

Thanks to Andrea for sitting down and talking gambling with me.

Thanks to Walt, Steve, Lindsey, Danny and Jerry for being there.

Thanks to Bonnie, this wouldn't have gotten done without you.

Pete Rose – baseball's all-time hit king. The man who played hard all the time. The man who never quit on an at-bat. The first player I would pick if I were drafting an all-time team. Pete Rose deserves to be in baseball's Hall of Fame based on what he was as a player. Whatever happened afterwards should remain separate from his playing career.

TABLE OF CONTENTS

WHY SPORTS GAMBLE?

Whether we like it or not, we've all been exposed to gambling from a very early age. From games of chance at kids' carnivals to church bingo, to dominoes, dice and card games. Even fund raising raffles. Gambling is all around us. It has been around in some form or another since the beginning of mankind.

And if you're going to gamble, many see sports gambling as a much greater value than traditional casino games. A hand of blackjack is over with quickly. A lot of money can leave your hands quickly. When you place a bet on a sporting contest, you usually have a few days to wonder about it. Then during the game you can have hours of entertainment. Sometimes right down to the last few seconds.

Most sports betters grew up watching and playing sports. They feel they have an acquired knowledge and judgment about the subject. They can relate easier than say betting on the stock market. With sports gambling the little guy or gal can be just as competent as the pro. There are lots of compelling reasons people sports gamble. Mostly because we're fans and we like following sports.

Young, old, professional, blue collar, guys, gals, all walks of life. Rich or poor, sports gambling transcends society.

Sports gambling can be many things -- legal entertainment, fun, profitable, dangerous, bankrupting, and sometimes criminal. It's *life*.

Why do people like to bet on sports? Why do people like to do anything that's a little on the edge? It's fun, it's exciting, it's risky, it's stimulating. With sports gambling, it's predicting the future of sorts. It's matching your wits with the experts. Some people say they feel as if they are part of the game because, in a way, they are competing.

There are scads of different ways to place a bet --

point spreads, futures, money lines, propositions all

tailored to one's personal taste. Sports gambling is

available year-round. One can bet on football, basketball,

baseball, NASCAR, golf, and more. The sports gambler

has a sense of control. At least the smart ones do.

Also, society has become more accepting of sports

gambling. It is seen less as an unsavory underworld

operation. It has become more mainstream. Most people

polled have no problem with legal gambling. There are

many good, hardworking, smart, honest people who like to

gamble on sports.

With all the crap that goes on today -- with pop

culture being what it is, with corrupt governments spending

out of control, with CEO's gutting companies (and getting

away with it), with oil and pharmaceutical companies

gouging the public, with our military being told to fight

wars with one hand tied behind it's back, with all the crap

that goes on in today's world, heck – sports gambling is *tame* by comparison.

In the information age in which we live, sports gambling has become more convenient. One can place bets from the privacy of the home using the internet. Scores of **off-shore sportbooks** have sprung up in recent years. There is a wealth of information out there for the public. There is the explosion of **sports radio**, with constant scores and information being broadcast. There are great TV packages, whether it be cable or satellite, that allow subscribers to watch virtually any game. Newsstands sell all kinds of magazines, newspapers, and stat sheets. There are plenty of **tout services**, all willing to sell you their picks. I personally do not recommend tout services, but to each his own. You don't have to look far to find the world of sports, nor the world of sports gambling. One thing is for sure, there are plenty of people gambling on sports. In 2004 there was a documented *$900 million* bet on football games alone. This is legal, regulated gambling. Imagine what the totals would be if you include the internet and illegal gambling. The 2006 Super Bowl set a record of *$95.5 million* legally bet. It's anybody's guess what the totals are. Some estimates are up to $10 billion. All this makes sports gambling the number one form of gambling.

I don't see it slowing down anytime soon. Governments are always looking for revenue streams and it may only be a matter of time before more states legalize it. There is a small percentage of compulsive gamblers who will never be satisfied, and will bet on anything. Compulsive gambling is not good. But then compulsive anything usually isn't good. With gambling there is always the lure of easy money. Some desperate people are trying to get out of a hole. For the most part, people sports gamble because they want to, and they can. Supply and demand.

I wrote this book in part because I'm amazed at the popularity of casinos, on-line poker, state lotteries, and gambling in general. Build a casino and they will come. There seems to be no shortage of people who want to gamble.

THINGS YOU MUST KNOW

THINGS YOU **MUST** KNOW

One term that all sports gamblers need to understand is the word **"Juice"** -- also known as the **"Vig"** or **"Vigorish."** Most novice gamblers think that if you bet $100 that you either win or lose $100. Not so! All **sportbooks** or private **bookies** charge a commission of roughly 10%. This is based on the standard 11/10 odds sports betting gives you. This is the sportbook's fee for setting up the system that allows you the privilege of placing your bets. The juice covers the **house** or bookies' cost of doing business and gives them a profit for their trouble.

Most legal gambling houses take the 10% from the winning side of the bet. So, if you bet $100 and lost, you would lose $100. If you bet $100 and won, you would get back your original $100 plus $90 in winnings, totaling $190, not the $200 one might expect.

Some illegal bookies will take the 10% from the losing side of the bet. So that if you bet $100 and lose, you would owe $110 and if you bet $100 and won, you would be credited $100 to your account. This difference is mostly because with legal gambling, you have to place the money up front before the bet is placed. In an illegal bookie operation, credit is usually extended to the bettor and they can place bets while being expected to either pay-up or collect on a **settle-up day** after the game bet on has been played.

This is all part of the **house edge** and can be frustrating and confusing. So that there are no surprises, you need to ask the house or the bookie what juice system they use. One must calculate the juice on any bet where you pick one side or the other.

As of this writing there are three ways to sports gamble if you live in the United States. The three ways are legal, sort of legal, and definitely illegal. It's the illegal side of sports gambling that the police, authorities and some of society have the big problem with. The illegal sports bookie has been around longer than legal gambling and operates under a different culture. With legal sports betting you must pay for your bet up front with real money. You can't bet it if you don't have it. With legal, everything is regulated by **state commissions**. There is a certain transparency that allows very little room for fraud and **fixes**. The illegal side is different. Most bookies operate by extending credit and taking bets over the phone or through third parties. A gambler may end up owing far more than they are capable of paying. There is a culture of squeezing the **debtor**. If you can't pay the cash, then maybe they'll take the car, diamond ring or plasma TV. Perhaps, if an athlete, coach or manager is in trouble with illegal gambling, they may be tempted to **throw a game** to make good with the bookies.

Not everyone lives near a legal sportsbook where the betting is legal and regulated. Not everyone is comfortable sports gambling over the internet which is somewhat legal and somewhat regulated. I say somewhat because the internet is a hard place to enforce jurisdiction and not all the overseas countries where the sportsbooks are based regulate much. The official rule in this country is that it is illegal to place a bet over a phone line. Not everyone is comfortable gambling illegally, but it may be their only option. One should know, however, that people can and have gone to jail over illegal sports gambling. In extreme cases, people end up losing everything and sometimes end up in the river or the local landfill. Money is a touchy subject that can bring out the worst in people. One should use wisdom and caution especially with the illegal side of sports gambling.

Rome wasn't built in a day. Like any good business or vocation, sports gambling takes work, patience, experience, discipline and good judgment. Luck and intuition will only take you so far. To be successful at sports gambling, you have to be good, and it helps to be lucky. Don't count on quick, easy money.

Let's do some quick math. Let's say you bet $100 each on five football games. Let's say you win three and lose two. Your take would look like this:

Game 1	Game 2	Game 3	Game 4	Game 5
Start $100	Start $100	Start $100	Start $100	Start $100
Win $90	Lose $100	Win $90	Lose $100	Win $90
Total $190	0	Total $190	0	Total $190

Total take for the five games: $570 ($70 to the good)

If you substitute $1,000 for the $100 bet, you would net a $700 profit for the five game bet. If you continued betting $100 per game on five games each week and averaged winning three out of five, (which is better than most people average) using this model over the course of a 15-week football season, you would net a $1,050 profit.

If you bet $1,000 instead of $100, you would net a profit of $10,500. So, depending on your price range, you would be earning a little more than a 20% profit. Not bad, but winning three of five is an optimistic model. So goes the lure of **parlays, teasers**, and high odds money lines and **future bets**. You have a chance to win a lot more money quickly. Actually, gamblers rarely win these bets, that's why sportsbooks love them.

It's better to be consistent. Nothing worthwhile comes easily. If you have the dedication and a healthy rational love of sports, and don't expect too much too soon, then you might be one of the few sports gamblers who profit.

Know how and who sets the **point spread** or **money line**. They are known as the **oddsmakers**. Usually they are based at the large sportsbooks in Las Vegas casinos. They have charts, stat computer print outs, all kinds of information. They usually come to a consensus of several people. You should know that the point spread or money line is set only to try to split the betting public. This is why the line moves up or down sometimes. The oddsmaker wants even action on both sides of the bet. The oddsmaker has no interest in predicting the actual score of the game. For example, if more money is being bet on a **favorite**, the oddsmaker will give a point or two to the **underdog** to try to entice people to bet on the underdog to even up the **action**. If there is even money bet on both sides of a bet then the bookmaker is guaranteed a profit no matter who wins the game because of the 10% juice they collect. This is how sports gambling operates. They are trying to split the gambling public, not predict the score. It is important to have early and late access to as many **betting lines** as possible. This will enable you to keep up with, or get a jump on line movement.

Sports gambling can be wonderful entertainment, casual curiosity, even professionally profitable. You should also know that, like any form of gambling, sports gambling can get people in a lot of trouble. **Moderation** and self-control are the key to avoid becoming one of the 2% of all adults who are helplessly addicted to gambling.

The legal age a person can be to place a sports bet in this country is 18. I would think anyone under the age of 18 should not be gambling his or her limited amount of income on any form of gambling. As far as adults are concerned, some people drink, some people raise horses, some people build and race cars. It's all entertainment which cost money. To each his own, but good judgment and self-control must be employed if you don't want to end up in the poorhouse, or in the river. People have lost everything – their homes, their families, their dignity, and social lives. There are plenty of people out there who are more than willing to take your money. Don't become a victim. Enjoy the wonderful world of sports gambling but tread lightly until you have become more experienced.

Know that the **house, sportsbook,** or **bookie** can, at any time, refuse to accept your **action**. It is a privilege and not a *right* to be able to sports gamble. They set the lines and they can set **limits** on the size of the bet. They can send you down the road if you become too good. No equal opportunity here. It's all part of the **house edge** that you are up against.

Some pro's will employ a person known as a **beard,** a frontperson who places someone else's bet as if it is his/her own. This isn't always easy because the pro needs to share some of the winnings with the beards, and sooner or later the beards/pro relationship could be exposed. It is best to have more than just a couple of places in which to sports gamble to give *yourself* a bit of an edge.

HOW AND WHERE TO SPORTS GAMBLE

HOW AND WHERE TO SPORTS GAMBLE

There are a few different choices a person has if they want to place bets on sporting events. They are all a little different, and they all have advantages and disadvantages over each other.

The internet is probably the most scientific and advantageous to the profit-minded sports gambler. **Line shopping** is easier and you have several choices and options from one seat. However, the internet can be undependable and confusing sometimes, and there is no human element involved.

Having a **bookie** has been the most common practice for sports gambling. The internet is changing this, but for many years all over the country, people have used bookies. People enjoy going out to their local bar, newsstand or meeting their friends who work at the local establishments and placing bets on sports. Not to mention all the office pools and Super Bowl boards. The practice, however, is unregulated and illegal which can cause multiple problems.

The state of **Oregon** currently sells a pro football **parlay ticket**. This, however, is limited and is actually supposed to cease and desist after the 2006-07 football season. Then there are the legal **sportbooks** in the state of **Nevada**. Most are located in one of the state's many casinos. This is regulated and generally on the up and up. This is face-to-face betting. You can even have complimentary drinks and watch the games on multiple TV screens in a great sports crowd *atmosphere*. Not everyone lives near Nevada, however, and some people don't like crowds or casinos.

Let's Start With **Nevada**.

The state of Nevada has over 150 registered

sportbooks spread throughout the state. Most are in the Las

Vegas or Reno areas. Smaller cities also have some casinos

with sportbooks located in them all around the state. If you

come to the Las Vegas area, here are some casino

sportbooks that come highly recommended:

Circus Circus sportbook
The **Monte Carlo**
Las Vegas **Hilton** sport book
Mandalay Bay
Green Valley Station (in Henderson)
Ballys/Paris race track and sportsbook
The Luxor
Star Dust Las Vegas
The Palms

If you can make it to Nevada but not Las Vegas,

you can call **(702) – 486- 2000** or visit

www.gaming.N.V.Gov and inquire where the nearest sport

book is in that area.

Not all sportbooks offer betting on every sporting

event. Some limit more than others. One thing they all have

in common is that they all want your business. Some will lavish their patrons with food and drink. Most all have multiple TV screens and pleasant seating. They have large boards showing **odds, point spreads,** and all the bets available to you. Like a racetrack, they have multiple windows to take the crowds' bets. Most casinos require cash bets at their windows, but some will extend credit to credit worthy individuals. Most have ATM's available if you don't want to carry around too much cash at once. You walk in, check out the game board, place your bets if you like the **lines** and then watch the games in a fun sports mad *atmosphere*. It would be wise if you have the ability to check out a few different sportbooks to see all of your options. The casinos are constantly evolving and upgrading. The only way to find out which sportbook is best for you is to experience them first hand.

Advantages

- Great sports *atmosphere*
- Complimentary food and drink

- Regulated gambling (at least you'll know you're going to get a pay out.)
- Immediate payouts (future bets can be mailed in.)
- No need to open multiple accounts
- Face to face people betting

Disadvantages

- Line shopping is difficult (although the Las Vegas casinos are in close proximity, by the time you go from one casino to another the line may have changed – and no cell phones are allowed).
- Sometimes can be annoying and too crowded.
- Sometimes the complimentary treats are funded by charging extra juice
- Not everyone can simply come to Nevada.

Now Let's Talk About **Oregon**

Oregon has sold a **pro football parlay ticket** since 1989. In part because of pressure from pro football and the **NCAA**, this form of sports gambling will no longer be available after the 2006-07 football season. It may survive however and until it's gone, you can purchase these tickets anywhere in the state of Oregon. Anywhere that it is where they sell lottery tickets such as gas stations, grocery stores or newsstands. Like any parlay ticket, you must bet multiple games. In Oregon you must bet at least three games on up to 14 games. You must win all the games you bet to win. The minimum bet is $2. If you win a three-game parlay you win $5 for every $1 you bet. If you win a four-game parlay you win $10 for every $1 you bet. If you win a five-game or more parlay you win a portion of the total pot that was bet that week. Tickets can only be bought in Oregon. Winning tickets up to $600 can be cashed in at any Oregon lottery retail location. Winnings over $600 must be cashed in at the lottery office in Salem Oregon. You can also mail in your winning tickets to:

P.O BOX 14515
Salem Oregon

If you want to be updated on the Oregon pro football parlay tickets, you can call the Oregon Lottery at (503) 540-1000.

Advantages

- Convenient easy purchase

- Regulated guaranteed payout
  Disadvantages

- Parlays are low percentage bets
- Limited to pro football
- May not be around much longer

Let's Talk About **Bookies**

Where there is money to be made there will always be people setting up shop. **Bookies** can be found in all walks of society -- school systems, fire departments, blue collar, even government agencies. The common interest in sports, the element of risk, and a chance for profit draws people to the bookie/gambler relationship. Bookies can range from inept and sloppy to sophisticated and professional. It may take a while to find one who is fair and competent. A good bookie is a good businessman. They offer a variety of bets, they pay on time, they make no excuses, they are clear and consistent. On the flip side, you should treat your bookie with the same professionalism. Having a good relationship with your bookie is essential to your sports gambling experience. If you can, try to have more than one good bookie that you can depend on. That way you have more access to different lines and more variety of bets. If you don't know of any bookies or where to find one, it never hurts to simply ask. Ask friends, ask co-workers, ask family members, ask contractors, ask business associates. You can also attend local sporting events such as high school or college games - even youth sports *(a dad whose kid is on my son's hockey team is a bookie).* Do a little socializing, be patient, be sincere, be assertive but not pushy, and chances are you'll find a bookie to place sports bets with. College frat houses are fertile bookmaking grounds. Golf country clubs, YMCA's, recreational softball and basketball leagues can offer leads. Even if you don't drink alcohol, you could go to the local corner bars as well as the big sports bars in the area. A measure of sports knowledge, politeness, and self-confidence can go a long way. Unless you live in extremely rural America, finding a bookie should not be that difficult.

Once you have found a bookie or two, you need to find out how they operate. You will usually be given a number or an alias to identify yourself with. You need to find out the bookie's schedule. What bets are offered, and when? When and where is **settle up day**? Can you stop by and place bets in person or do they use phones or computers? Most good bookies want your business because they make money off of gamblers. Once you get the hang of it, the bookie's system will become simplistic to you. Like people, no two bookies are exactly alike. This is unregulated territory and anything can happen. Many of bookies have come and gone. No one does it forever. Usually they are people who used to sports gamble and got tired of losing money. Illegal or not, as long as there are people who want to bet on sports, there will be people setting up shop as bookies.

Advantages

- Local, usually convenient gambling
- Fun social gambling
- Credit is usually extended
- No need to set up new bank accounts

Disadvantages

- It's illegal. If your bookies get busted, he may take you with him
- Sometimes limited betting
- Unregulated – your bookie may leave town with your winnings
- Sometimes associated with a dark subculture; you could get in over your head.

Office Pools and Super Bowl Boards

Office pools and boards can be fun for the casual gambler, but they are limited and not very scientific. During football season, a **parlay ticket** may be distributed throughout the work place. As we have said, these bets are difficult to win, and you may be limited to only parlays. Sometimes the people who run these tickets and pools are very amateur. Mistakes are made and there are communication breakdowns. I know of one time my wife brought home a college football parlay from her place of employment at a local school district. The ticket displayed 10 or so games with favorites and underdogs clearly noted. I made my picks accordingly. Well come to find out, this parlay only wanted you to pick the winners with no consideration to the point spread. I thought to myself, then why display the point spread? How amateur.

March madness brackets and **Super Bowl boards**, Nascar and other boards can be found at bars, diners, auto repair shops, all over. With the exception of March madness brackets, these are potluck wagers that have little to do with skill or sports knowledge. *You don't even know what numbers you have* until the board is filled up. **March madness** brackets are distributed around offices and the same places that you will find Super Bowl boards. You try to predict the fate of 64+ teams. This is a little more skillful, but the combinations and possibilities make this play very difficult. If you want to have a little fun and not spend a lot of time and money, then there is little harm in these bets, you might get lucky! The winners usually get a portion of the pot, which is divided up accordingly. There is no bookie or house squeezing off any juice. The cops view this as harmless and generally don't bust people, but the possibility remains.

Advantages

- Convenient low-cost gambling
- Little homework or research needed
- No need to open new accounts or credit cards

Disadvantages

- Limited low percentage bets
- Inconsistent availability
- Amateurish in nature

How About the Internet?

Anyone who has access to an unfiltered internet connection can now routinely, relatively easily bet on sporting events. There are dozens of **off-shore sportbooks** on the internet. Like casinos, they all operate a little differently. Some want you to use only credit cards, some want you to start an account with them and only want to credit your account when you win, forcing you to make withdrawals which isn't always easy. Most all offer a variety of bets in the usual sports. Some sportbooks also offer regular casino gambling. Some internet sportbooks are scams offering deals that are too good to be true.

The best thing that you can do, if you want to gamble over the internet, is to *plan ahead and do a little research*. You will also have to budget your bankroll into a few different accounts. Some sportbooks will try to entice you to use a credit card by offering a sign-up bonus and immediate betting. You don't want to use your main credit card. The one that you use for family and business. Nor do you want to use a limited $500 card. Some credit cards will not deal with any gambling establishments. Even if you win, some cards will not accept any credits from a sportsbook. Don't use the $500 card because it would always be maxed, thus hurting your credit score.

As of October 2006, President Bush signed a law that bans the use of credit cards, checks and electronic transfers for internet gambling. The popular website betonsports.com among others were shut down. Their customers had their accounts frozen and may never get their money back. Some of the website executives have been brought up on charges. This has put somewhat of a dent in online gambling. This law is not uniformly enforced however. Once again, the internet is a gray area. As of this writing, you can still find **off short sportbooks** who use banks and processors who will let you use a credit card, or wire transfer. You have to shop around and ask questions.

What you want to do is to look for sportbooks that accept deposits in their start-up accounts in the form of **money orders** or **Western Union** transfers. Set this up before you want to start betting. This is the account that you will bet off of. The sportbook will take your losses from this account. It is up to you to keep track of and replenish these accounts. Limit your deposits to $500 or so. Don't give them everything at once. This is not immediate, but it's still pretty quick. Plus it limits your risk. Ideally, these same sportbooks will pay out your winnings by mailing you a check or money order. Some may want to use Western Union and pay out to a bank account. You can start a small ($200) account. This should be a new separate account, not the one you have had since the 7th grade. The sportbook can't withdrawal from this account. They do that from the money order accounts that you set up with them.

An ideal situation would be to have accounts with 3-4 sportbooks. This would enable you to **line shop** and have access to a wider variety of bets. They could all transfer your winnings to the same single bank account or mail you your winnings. Remember – set this up *before* you want to start gambling.

In researching your choices of sportbooks, you may find an annoying amount of information. Be patient and diligent. There are scams out there and you must keep your guard up. Here are some internet sportbooks that come highly recommended.

www.VIPsports.com
www.PinnacleSport.com
www.Sportsbook.com
www.diamond.com
www.Bowmans.com
www.Nine.com
www.SportsInteraction.com
www.MyBookie.com

Most of these websites also have 800 numbers so you can call to clarify any questions. You can simply type in the words offshore Sportbooks, you'll get plenty of leads. One website you might want to research is www.sportintensity.com. They have a lot of recommendations as well as a black list of sportbooks that you want to stay away from.

Advantages

- Quick access to many bets and many lines.

- Shop to get the very best line.
- Gamble from the privacy of your home or office.

Disadvantages

- Need to set up an account for various accounts.
- Must be somewhat computer savvy.
- Power outages and website crashes.
- Technically illegal.

ALL SPORTS

ALL SPORTS

Football

Football is the undisputed king of the sports gambling world. Professional football slightly edges college football in terms of popularity. The best bet you can make with football is a simple straight bet, one *individual game* at a time. Each game is usually **handicapped** by **a point spread**, where one team is **favored** over the other which is the **underdog**. The **line** is expressed like this:

Favored	Pts.		Underdog
Colts	4	vs.	Dolphins
Sea Hawks	3	vs.	Cowboys

Let's take the Colts-Dolphins game. If you bet on the Colts, they must win by more than four points for you to win your bet. If you bet on the Dolphins, they must either win the game, or lose by three or less points for you to win your bet. If the difference is four points, say 24-20 Colts win, then the bet is a **push** and all money is returned.

Think of the Dolphins as starting with a four-point head start, or just add four points to the Dolphin's final score. If the actual final score is Colts 17 – Dolphins14, then for gambling purposes the score would be Dolphins 18 – Colts 17. **Underdogs** don't always win the actual game, but they win about 60% of the time when a **point spread** is factored in.

Sometimes when two teams are judged equal, then the **line** will be expressed as **pick-em**. This means that there is no **point spread**, you simply choose which team you think will win.

Along with the **point spread**, there sometimes is a **total** number on which you can bet the **over/under**. It is expressed like this:

Favored	Pts.	Over/Under	Underdog
Colts	4	30 vs.	Dolphins
Sea Hawks	3	34 vs.	Cowboys

You can bet on whether both the Colts and Dolphins total points will add up to either **over** or **under** 30 points. If we stay with the score of Colts 17 – Dolphins 14, then the total is 31. If you bet the **over** you win. Bet the **under** you lose. If the total hit exactly 30, then all bets would be a **push** and all money would be returned. This model applies to all football – pro, college, arena or any other league. Rarely, but sometimes you will find a football **moneyline** bet. It is expressed like this:

Favorite		Underdog
Colts -130	vs.	Dolphins +120
Sea Hawks –120	vs.	Cowboys +110

All **moneyline** bets are based on the number 100. If you take the favorite you risk more money to win less. Meaning, if you bet on the Colts, you must bet $130 to try to win $100. If the colts win, then you win $100 plus you get your $130 back for a total of $230. If you take the **underdog** Dolphins, you must bet $100 to try to win $120. If the Dolphins win, you win $120 plus get your $100 back for a total of $220. If your team loses, you lose what you bet. The team you take must only win the game, with no

point spread involved. As most always, there is some **juice** charged.

Parlays are common throughout society during football season. This is where anyone from an amateur to large **casino** will offer **parlay** tickets or sheets. A **parlay** is where you must win two or more games in combination. The higher the number of games bet, the greater the pay-out. *This is tempting, but parlays are not considered good gambling.* If you take a three game **parlay** and win two games but lose one, then you lose the entire bet. Win two games and **push** one, then your payout is reduced. **Teasers** are similar in which you must win games in combination, but you are given extra points to try to entice you to take this bet. The catch is the payout is reduced and you still have to win all the games to win your bet. *It is tough enough to win one game let alone more in combination.* It is much smarter to bet one game at a time.

Futures are popular where you try to pick how a team will do before the season starts. **Futures** are expressed like this:

<u>Odds to Win Super Bowl</u>

Patriots 4 - 1
Giants 8 – 1

Meaning, if you bet $100 on the Patriots, you are trying to win $400. If they win the Super Bowl, you get your $100 back plus $400 in winnings.

There are **futures over/unders** expressed like this:

Nebraska   8 wins
L.S.U.   9 wins

Meaning that you can choose whether Nebraska will win more or less than 8 games for the season. If they win exactly eight games, then your bet is a **push** and all money is returned. There are **exotic over/unders** such as how much yardage a certain running back will get in a game, or how much yardage a quarter back will throw for the year.

There are kinds of bizarre **exotics** – anything from which team will win the coin toss, to who will get the first sack. It is best to stay away from these bets along with **reverses, buying points** or any other sucker bets.

At the conclusion of football season, it is hard not to stumble across a **Super Bowl board** or two. As mentioned throughout this book, this isn't very scientific gambling. It's more like a lottery, maybe with a little better odds. You have to hope you get good numbers and then hope both teams hit them. If you win a **Super Bowl board**, you're simply lucky. Have fun if you like, but don't count on being lucky.

Football is a wonderful American sport which draws a lot of gambling interest. Enjoy all levels of football for the great sport that it is.

Basketball

College basketball's **March Madness** is probably the most widespread gambling on basketball. The NBA play-offs are a distant second. **March Madness** is the most common but hardly the best sport bet. It is usually small stakes and you have to predict the fate of 64+ teams. You have to be really good *and* lucky to get even close when filling out your brackets. There are surprises and upsets and disappointments and just too many games to call in one play. Have fun if you wish but don't put much hope into this tournament.

Basketball probably has the most *availability* of any sport. There are thousands of college and pro games played each season. Women's basketball actually gets some **action**. Powerhouse college programs such as Tennessee and Connecticut have brought some interest to their sport. This is actually good for the sports gambler. The **oddsmakers** can't possibly **handicap** all the games as closely as they do football for example. A good gambler can take advantage of this by studying less popular teams and games, maybe capitalizing in places where the **house** doesn't expect it. *One series or one game at a time.*

Like football, most basketball games are **handicapped** by a **point spread**. Example:

Favorite	Pts.		Underdog
North Carolina	7-1/2	vs.	Connecticut
Oregon	5	vs.	Stanford

If you pick North Carolina, they must win by 8 or more points. If you pick Connecticut they must win the game, or lose by 7 or less points. Sometimes when the score hits at exactly the **points spread**, then the game is a **push**, all money is returned. Sometimes there are **point spreads** for each half or all four quarters of a game.

You can also bet the **over/under** on the total number of points scored by both teams added up.

Example:

Favorite	Pts.	Over/Under	Underdog
North Carolina	7-1/2	149 vs.	Connecticut
Oregon	5	160 vs.	Stanford

If the final score is North Carolina 77, Connecticut 74, then the total is 151. If you bet **over** you win. If you bet **under** you lose.

There are **parlays** and **teasers** and **exotics**. As we have said, these are not good bets. It is okay to bet on a series, however, taking one side or the other. One thing professional basketball provides are play-off series. You gamble not on one game, but who will win a best of 5 or best of 7 game play-off series. It is usually expressed in **odds** or **moneylines**. Example:

Favorite	Odds	Underdog
Lakers	6 to 5	Kings

Meaning, if you want to bet on the Lakers, you must bet 6 dollars to try to win 5 dollars. If you want the Kings, you bet 5 dollars to try to win 6. You can bet whatever the **limit** is, but it will be based on the 6 to 5 **odds**.

Sometimes you will find a **moneyline** bet which is based on 100. It will be expressed like this:

<u>Favorite</u>		<u>Underdog</u>
Lakers –120	vs.	Kings +110

Meaning, if you want the Lakers, you must bet $120 to try to win $100 or if you want the Kings you bet $100 to try to win $110. Sometimes when one team is significantly better than another, such as a #1 seed vs. a #8 seed, you will see a large **moneyline** such as:

<u>Favorite</u>		<u>Underdog</u>
Heat –280	vs.	Knicks +240

This is still based on 100, but the stakes are much higher. If you want the Heat, you must bet $280 to try to win $100, or if you want the Knicks, you bet $100 to try to win $240. Sometimes, when a team is really superior to another, the **house** will give odds on whether or not the series will be a 4-0 sweep. Some **juice** is charged, of course.

At the start of the season, there are the standard **future** bets. **Odds** on who will win the NCAA or the NBA championships. Example:

> **Odds** to win NBA championship
> San Antonio Spurs   5-1
> Miami Heat   8-1

Meaning if you bet the Spurs, for every one dollar you bet, you're trying to win 5. If you bet $1,000 and they win the championship, you would win $5,000 plus your original $1,000.

Then there are **future over/unders**. Example:

> LA Lakers   48
> Detroit Pistons   46

This total is for the regular season. If you think that the Lakers will win more than 48 games bet **over**. If you think the Lakers will win less than 48 games, bet **under**. If they win exactly 48 games, then the bet is a **push** and all money is returned.

There are any number of **exotics** and **propositions** such as who will win the rebounding title, or how many times a certain coach will get ejected. These can get really bizarre and are best to stay away from.

Basketball offers a unique opportunity for the savvy sports gambler. It fills a void after football season and draws decent gambling **action**.

Baseball

Baseball is one team sport where one person (*the pitcher*) largely influences the **betting line**. An ace pitcher who is hot will usually trump a good team as far as the **oddsmakers** are concerned. Previous games circumstances, winning and losing streaks, even umpires will influence. There are plenty of games from April through late October and the College World Series gets some **action**.

The listed starting pitchers must start for each team for the bet to be honored. If for some reason one of the pitchers is scratched, then the bet is considered **no action** and all money is returned.

Most baseball bets are expressed as **odds** or **moneyline** bets. Example:

Favorite	Odds		Underdog
Cubs	7 to 5	vs.	Mets

If you want the Cubs, you must bet 7 dollars to try to win 5, or $70 to try to win $50 and so on. If you want the Mets, you bet 5 dollars to try to win 7 or $50 to try to win $70 and so on, all based on the 7 to 5 **odds**. Some juice is charged, usually to the winning **underdog's** side.

More common is a **moneyline** bet based on 100 such as:

Favorite		Underdog
Cubs –130	vs.	Mets +115

Meaning, if you want the Cubs, you must risk $130 to try to win $100. If you want the Mets, you bet $100 to try to win $115. You can bet any amount you like but it will be based proportionally on this model. The **favorite** is penalized not by **points spread** but by the amount of money risked vs. the amount to be won. Sometimes if a team is a heavy **favorite** you will see a **line** like:

Favorite	Underdog
Yankees –260	Royals +230

Being still based on 100, if you want the Yankees, you must risk $260 to try to win $100 and if you like the Royals, you bet $100 to try to win $230.

Like some other sports, you can bet on baseball's post season play-offs. This is where you bet on who will win a best of 5 or best of 7 game series. The same principles apply as with **moneyline** and **odds** bets, except that you're betting on a whole series, and not just a single game.

There are **future** bets such as who will win the World Series.

Example:

Odds to win World Series

New York Yankees   4-1

LA Dodgers   8-1

Meaning, if you think that the Yankees will win the World

Series, you are trying to win 4 dollars for every 1 dollar

that you bet.

There are **future over/unders** where you try to

predict how many games a particular team will win in the

regular season. Example:

Boston Red Sox   85
Cincinnati Reds   79

If you think the Red Sox will win more than 85

games, bet **over**. If you think the Red Sox will win less

than 85, bet **under**. If the Red sox win exactly 85 games,

the bet is a **push** and all money is returned.

Sometimes you will see an **over/under** for total

runs scored between both teams. If the final score is

Phillies 8, Braves 7, then the total would be 15. You

simply bet either **over** or **under** whether you think the

teams will score more or less than the posted number.

There is what is known as a **run line** bet that combines a **points spread** and a **moneyline**. You want to stay away from these bets just like **parlays, teasers** and the rest of the sucker bets. The teams are already handicapped by the **moneyline** and now your team has to win by a **point spread** also. You essentially have to win two bets in one play. Bet one or the other but not both.

Home plate umpires can make a huge difference. An umpire with a larger strike zone which favors pitchers can reduce the offense, thus reducing the **over/under**. Some umpires squeeze the strike zone forcing the starting pitchers to work harder and longer. Thus allowing teams to get into each other's bullpens sooner, forcing the total runs upward. Certain umpires or crews sometimes have a history good or bad with certain teams. Keep an eye on the umpires who you think call the game incorrectly. You can know who is scheduled to umpire home plate prior to making your bet. Major league baseball.com has a lot of information. Also your local newspaper sports department can be very helpful.

Sometimes games are shortened or rained out. A game must be considered an official game at its conclusion for all bets to be honored.

Hockey

Hockey is sort of a large cult sport that lately hasn't gotten the love that it deserves. One reason is that it is a far greater sport to watch in person rather than on television. Also, if you take a look at the top 20 NHL scorers, you would be lucky to pronounce 7 names correctly. It's sometimes hard for the average sports gambler to relate. There are some good bets however. National interest picks up as the play-offs begin, also during Olympic years.

The most common hockey bet is a **moneyline** bet.

Example:

<u>Favorite</u>   <u>Underdog</u>
Lightning –155   vs.   Rangers +140

Canadians −140   vs.   Maple Leafs +130

Meaning, if you bet on the Lightning, you would bet $155 to try to win $100. If you want to bet on the Rangers, you would bet $100 to try to win $140. As we have said about the **moneyline** being based on 100, you can bet any amount you want, but it will be proportional to these numbers. As always, some **juice** will be charged.

There are **over/unders** for goals scored, such as:

Favorite	Over/Under		Underdog
Lightning −155	6	vs.	Rangers +140

If both teams combined to score more than 6 goals then the **over** bet wins. If they score less than 6, then the **under** bet wins. If they score exactly 6 goals, then the bet is a **push** and all money is returned.

If a team is heavily favored, you may see a large **moneyline** such as:

Favorite		Underdog
Penguins −250	vs.	Blue Jackets +230

This is still based on 100. If you bet the Penguins, you must bet $250 to try to win $100 and if you want the Blue Jackets, you bet $100 to try to win $230.

There are a lot of games and a lot of travel. Even very good teams lose to bad teams once in a while. You have to look at circumstances. Maybe a team is due to rest its top goalie, or maybe they're coming off a long flight delay. If you catch these high **odds underdogs** right, you can make some good money.

As with other team sports, you can bet on hockey play-off series. You bet on who will win a best of 5 or best of 7 game series, instead of just one game. Sometimes when one team is heavily favored, you might see **odds** on a 4-0 sweep. Such as:

Odds to Sweep

Favorite			Underdog
Devils	3 to 1	vs.	Flyers

Meaning, for every $1 you bet on the Devils to sweep, you are trying to win $3. If the Flyers win even just one game they become the winning side of the bet.

Sometimes you will see a **puck** or **Canadian line**. This is a combined **moneyline** *and* **point spread**. While this bet is still based on 100, it changes the bet from simple win or lose. Example:

Favorite		Underdog
Stars +1-1/2 – 150	vs.	Devils –1-1/2 +130

If you want the Stars, you must bet $150 to try to win $100, but they can still lose by less than two goals to win the bet. If you want the Devils, you bet $100 to try to win $130, but they have to win by two or more goals. You're still betting **moneyline** money but now the game is **handicapped** by a **point spread** also. In essence, this contest is **handicapped** twice. It would be wise to stay away from these type of bets, along with **parlays, teasers** and the rest of the gimmicks.

There are **future over/unders** ranging from the logical to the bizarre. You can bet on how many games a certain team will win in the regular season. Example:

	Over/Under
New Jersey Devils	65
Detroit Red Wings	59

If you think the Redwings will win more than 59 games, bet **over**. If you think the Devils will win less than 65 games, bet **under**. Then there are the bizarre **over/unders** such as how many penalty minutes a certain player will get. Or what the total attendance a team will get.

Hockey is a cold sport that can be very hot. There are many games providing plenty of opportunity to the sports gambler.

Auto Racing

While the Indy 500 and some Lemans events are still big races, NASCAR is currently the top dog of auto racing in the sports gambling world. NASCAR seems to attract a wider spectrum of fans. I guess anyone who drives a car can relate. Also in the case of NASCAR, all the drivers' names sound like someone you went to school with. The cars are American – Ford, Dodge and Chevy, although lately Toyota has joined the fray. The most basic bet is simply picking the winner of a race. Most **sportsbooks** will list 15-20 drivers along with the rest of the field like this:

Dale Earnhardt, Jr.	5-1
Jeremy Mayfield	11-1
Rest of Field	100-1

If you bet $100 on Dale Earnhardt, Jr. and he wins, you would win $500 plus get back your original $100 minus **juice**. If you bet $100 on someone in the field and they spring an upset to win, then you would win $10,000 plus your original $100 minus **juice**. Sometimes match up bets will be available where two drivers will be paired against each other in a **moneyline** bet. Example:

Favorite	Underdog
Jeff Gordon −150	Dale Jarrett +125

Whichever driver finishes higher wins the bet. Both drivers must start the race for the bet to be valid. As with all **moneyline** bets, these numbers are based on 100. If you want Jeff Gordon, you must bet $150 to try to win $100. If you want Dale Jarrett, you must bet $100 to win $125. You can bet any amount you want, but it will be proportional to these numbers.

There are **futures** in auto racing such as who will win the Formula One or Nextel Cup. Something like this:

Nextel Cup Championship

Tony Stewart	5-1
Kasey Kahne	7-1

If you think Tony Stewart will win the cup, than for every $1 you bet, you're trying to win $5. If you think that Kasey Kahne will win the cup, than for every $1 you bet, you're trying to win $7.

There are bizarre **futures** and **proposition** bets such as how many laps in a race before a yellow caution flag comes out. You can even bet on which automaker will win the race (Ford, Dodge, Chevy and Toyota).

Racing season runs from mid-winter to late fall and offers a nice alternative to the traditional team sports. You may find NASCAR boards around your community, but these are merely pot-luck bets where you don't know who you're betting on until you have already paid your money. You should be able to at least pick your driver.

Golf

Golf is becoming a popular sports bet. In general, people who golf tend to have more disposable income. Therefore, in theory, they would have more money to sports gamble. Country clubs are known sports gambling havens so why not bet on Golf also. Like NASCAR, the most common bet is simply picking the winner of a given tournament. Usually a **sportsbook** will list 30 or so golfers at various **odds** and the rest of the field at very long **odds.**

Example:

Tiger Woods	2-1
John Daly	10-1
Rest of Field	75-1

If you think that Tiger Woods is going to win, then for every $1 you bet, you're trying to win $2. If you bet $1,000 on Tiger and he wins, you win $2,000 plus you get back your original $1,000 for a total of $3,000 minus **juice.** If you think some unknown from the field might win, then for every $1 you bet, you would win $75. If you bet $100 on someone from the field and they win, then you would win $7,500 plus your original $100 for a total of $7,600 minus **juice.**

You might find a match-up **moneyline** bet where two golfers are paired against each other. Whoever finishes higher (with the lower score in golf) wins the bet.

Example:

Favorite	Underdog
Ernie Els –120	David Love III +110

The **moneyline** is based on 100 and if you want Ernie Els, you risk $120 to try to win $100. If you want Davis Love III, you risk $100 to try to win $110. You can bet any amount that you want, but it will be proportional to these numbers.

There are **propositions** and **futures** such as **odds** to who will be leading money winner or how many hole-in-ones if any will be recorded in a certain tournament.

Golf is becoming almost a year-round sport with the four majors being most bet upon. Women's golf with established stars such as Anika Sorenstam and Carrie Webb and young stars such as Paula Creamer have drawn interest to their sport. Golf, along with NASCAR are fast growing sports gambling sports.

Boxing

Boxing was once the king of the sports gambling world. It's golden era of the 70's and 80's were glorious years for the sport. The heavy weight championship was at one time the most coveted prize in sports. The sport had huge stars – Leonard, Hearns, Duran, Ali, Frazier, Mancini, Holmes, Foreman, plus many more. The difference between then and now is the sport used to get regular primetime television exposure. It's currently limited to cable and pay-per view, plus kids would rather play basketball or practice karate than box. After all Sonny Liston once said, *"You would have to be crazy to want to make a living getting hit upside of your head."* The sports popularity has declined, but there are still some bets to be made. Obviously the simplest bet is to pick the winner of a fight. You can do this with your buddy with no **bookie** involved. This is an old fashioned straight bet with no **juice** involved, you bet $100, you win or lose $100. As far as betting with a **casino** or **sportsbook** is concerned, you can usually find **odds** or **moneyline** bets. Example:

Favorite			Underdog
Tyson	45-1	vs.	Douglass

This was the actual **line** on this 1990 fight. If you thought Tyson would win, you would have to bet $45 to try to win $1. If you thought Douglass would win, for every $1 you bet, you would win $45. Douglass went on to win this fight in a huge upset and **odds** are usually never this long.

Sometimes you will find **moneyline** bets. Example:

Favorite		Underdog
Perez −160	vs.	Jones +145

With the **moneyline** being based on 100, if you want Perez, you must bet $160 to try to win $100. If you like Jones, you bet $100 to try to win $145. Whatever money you bet will be proportional to these numbers. Some **juice** will be taken.

There are **over/unders** such as how many rounds a fight will last. If a fight ends in a draw or tie, then the bet is considered a no contest and all money is returned.

Soccer

I guess this chapter wouldn't be complete without a section on soccer. This sport is a strong youth sport in this country. Soccer does generate a gambling interest when the World Cup comes around. Mostly you can find **moneyline** bets. Example:

Favorite		Underdog
Brazil –600	vs.	USA +550

Again, with the **moneyline** being based on 100. If you want Brazil, you must bet $600 to try to win $100. If you want the USA, you must bet $100 to try to win $550. You can bet whatever you like, but the numbers will be proportional to these. If the contest ends in a draw, then the bet is considered **no action** and all money is returned. You can, however, bet that the contest *will* end in a tie or draw.

Example:

France vs. Germany   Draw +400

Meaning, you bet $100 to try to win $400 if the game ends in a tie. If there are any penalty shots and an official winner is declared, then all draw bets are considered losing bets.

There are **over/under** bets for total goals scored.

Example:

Total 2-1/2

Meaning, if you think the total goals between both teams is going to be three or more, then bet **over**. If you think the total goals will be two or less, then bet **under**.

There are bizarre **proposition** bets such as will David Beckham kick a field goal for a NFL team, or how long will it be before he and his wife split.

Tip: Home countries or home teams always seem to do well for one reason or another. Keep this in mind.

TIPS AND STRATEGIES

GENERAL TIPS AND STRATEGIES

First staple. Always use your own judgment. There are plenty of **pundits** and **touts**. Some will sell you their knowledge and predictions with a lot of hyperbole. You see basically the same things they see. If you're interested and do your homework; if you watch games, pay attention and read a lot; if you form your own opinion and stick with it, you'll be a lot better off. You will still be wrong sometimes, but at least it was your calculated risk and not someone else's.

Do what is known as **paper trading** at first. Before wagering any real money, play or mock bet for a few weeks. Write down your bets and keep track of your record. See how you score, see if you would be winning or losing money. Once you're comfortable, you can dive in. Remember, you must win 53% of the time if you want to make a profit. Remember, even the very best of the best only win 60% of the time over the long haul. You might be good at this, you might not – that's a small margin.

Start with a set bankroll and never gamble with money you can't afford to lose. One rule of thumb is to only bet 2% of your bankroll on every individual bet, i.e., if you start with $5,000 then 2% would be $100. This may not seem like much but at least this will keep you playing through some dry spells. Only raise your bets when you are considerably ahead and never bet most or everything trying to get out of a hole. The best gamblers grind out the bookies over the long haul. Keep notes on your bets, review and learn from them.

If you go to a casino, leave the ATM and credit cards at home. Don't accept credit from the casino and watch what you drink. These old tricks have been going on for years and have gotten many people in trouble. Have a game plan and a clear head and you will fare much better.

In general, if you want to slant your gambling one way or the other, slant it toward the **underdog**. Underdogs win in sports gambling about 60% of the time. At least when there is a **point spread** involved. This is a documented fact. The only exception to this rule is in basketball where strong home courts, frequent games and frequent travel contribute to favorites winning more often. As a rule, gambling houses win because most people love favorites and are reluctant to pick underdogs. All games are different and you should make your picks individually, but underdogs have ruled for a long time.

Here is a sample from college football's 2005 Bowl season:

Favorite	Pts.	Underdog	Actual Score	Winning Bet
	Hawaii Bowl			
Nevada	1-1/2	Central Florida	Nevada 49/Central FL 48	Underdog
	Motor City Bowl			
Memphis	6	Akron	Memphis 38/Akron 21	Favorite
	Insight Bowl			
Arizona St.	12	Rutgers	Arizona St. 45/Rutgers 40	Underdog
	Mac Computers Bowl			
Boise St.	1	Boston College	Boston College 27/Boise St. 21	Underdog
	Alamo Bowl			
Michigan	13	Nebraska	Nebraska 28/Michigan 21	Underdog
	Emerald Bowl			
Georgia Tech	8	Utah	Utah 28 / Georgia Tech 10	Underdog
	Holiday Bowl			
Oregon	3	Oklahoma	Oklahoma 17/Oregon 14	Underdog
	Music City Bowl			
Minnesota	3	Virginia	Virginia 34/Minnesota 21	Push or Tie
	Sun Bowl			
UCLA	3-1/2	Northwestern	UCLA 50/Northwestern 38	Favorite
	Independence Bowl			
South Carolina	3-1/2	Missouri	Missouri 38 /South Carolina 31	Underdog

In the 2006 Bowl Season, underdogs won 17 games, favorites won 14 with one push.

If you really want to be a good gambler, then lay off parlays and teasers. These bets are house gimmicks where the pay-off is better, but the odds are much worse. Look at all games individually. It is much better to pick your bets on your own terms. Most good gamblers grind out their living.

Perhaps you should condense your focus and concentrate on specific sports, teams, divisions or conferences. In basketball and hockey, for example, there are far too many teams and games to really get a good read on everything. If you're familiar with only a couple of sports, maybe you should be content to only bet those sports. If you live in Canada, bet hockey. If you live in the Midwest, bet on the Big 10. Familiarity with your landscape is a valuable tool in any endeavor.

Bet with your head and not your heart. Take the emotion out of your betting. Avoid betting on a team just because they're your favorite. If it's a logical bet to go against your team, don't hesitate to do so.

Look for teams that are overrated. Early season lines tend to favor teams for what they did the previous year. During the season and late in the season look for teams that have overrated individuals on those teams. A couple of recent examples in baseball are Sammy Sosa and Barry Bonds. For a while Sammy was the toast of Chicago, and some people say Barry is the greatest player of our generation. Puh-leeez – these guys are great home run hitters, who, in my opinion, didn't help their teams win much. They were dreadful players defensively and for all their home runs, they didn't bat in that many runs. They were overrated, more flash than substance. I'd bet against those guys any day. The media tends to overrate certain teams and stars. Don't be afraid to go against popular thought.

Look at the upcoming schedule and try setting your own lines before the house lines come out. Compare your way of thinking to the house. If you feel strongly that they have made a mistake, you might consider betting that game. By betting your own lines, you won't be influenced in anyway except for your own judgment. After gaining some experience, this practice will become easier and you'll look forward to it.

When using the internet, avoid using your credit cards. It may seem quick and convenient for sports gambling purposes, but there are a lot of reasons not to use the credit cards. Some credit card companies won't deal with gambling establishments. Some may charge high fees for advances and draws. Your credit rating may be put at some risk. There is the temptation to overspend. Your name could go on multiple mail and call list, bringing all kinds of unwanted solicitations. Identity theft is a risk regardless of what anyone says about security. Cyber-criminals come up with something new everyday. What you should do is plan ahead and use **money orders** or **Western Union**. This helps keep you more anonymous and lessens your risk.

Don't feel compelled to have to make a bet. It's okay to let a whole week or two go by without gambling. Sometimes there just isn't anything worth buying or taking a chance on. The good gamblers don't just hope, they feel good about their bets, and make educated wagers.

I would recommend reading a variety of newspapers and publications, but if your only going to read one and one only, then **USA Today** is one of the most complete. Being a national newspaper, it has less local bias and negativity. It carries news from Las Vegas with most of the **betting lines**.

Future bets are generally not good bets. The World Series winners from 2002 through 2006 (the Angels, Marlins, Red Sox, White Sox, and Cardinals) were surprises that not many people had predicted. Prior to the NFL's 2006 season, many had predicted the Carolina Panthers to go to the Super Bowl. They didn't' even make the playoffs. Future odds are largely based on speculation and last year's results. Each new season is different from the past and is risky to judge.

If you live in an area with multiple colleges or pro teams, try to attend as many practices or team functions as you can. Be around, *check out how people act and what kind of character they have.* This may seem difficult especially with the pro or bigger college programs but sometimes it is easier than you think. Walk or jog around the track where the team is practicing. Play catch in the parking lot. Go have a drink where team members hang out. Observe things with your own two eyes. Sometimes a coach or player has a public persona that is different from his real one. I have seen this cut both ways. Good guy – bad reputation, bad guy – good reputation. The more you observe the better. It may change the way you would gamble on a team.

THE COPS

THE REFS

THE BEAUTIFUL WOMEN

THE COPS, THE REFS, THE BEAUTIFUL WOMEN

The Cops

As we have said, there are three ways to sports gamble -- legally in states such as Nevada and Oregon; somewhat legally over the internet with off-shore sports books; then illegally with an illegal bookmaker.

The cops don't need to police the legal gambling in Nevada and Oregon, it's policed by state gaming commissions and regulators. The cops don't seem to be too interested in internet gambling. The internet is a hard place to enforce jurisdiction. The official rule in this country is that it is illegal to place a bet over a telephone wire, thus making internet gambling illegal. Though like hitch-hiking and j-walking, this rule is rarely enforced. For now at least, the cops won't be knocking on your door if you sports gamble via the internet.

Where the cops come into play is when there is an illegal bookmaking operation going on. Most of society has no problem with gambling, but our government can act in strange ways sometimes.

Did you know that **Aljazeera**, the vile Arab TV network, the propaganda spout for radical Islam, the TV network that mysteriously doesn't know where their video tapes come from, the ones who inflame Arab hatred as a regular staple of their programming – did you know that Aljazeera is headquartered right down the road from the American Military headquarters based in the Persian Gulf country of Qatar? This is a double dealing agreement that the U.S. and Qatar governments have struck. We get to base our military hardware on their soil and for this we ignore their wanton spreading of Alqaeda propaganda. This is a lousy way to fight a war, but that's how our government works sometimes.

You might wonder why the cops would bother with illegal bookmaking when there is so much more serious violent crime going on. The cops are part of our government and the government picks and chooses what it is going to demonize. There are some legitimate concerns however. Some will tell you that sports gambling is not a victimless crime. For one thing, people are making a lot of untaxed money. There are untold millions being bet with no tax being collected. The government doesn't like this. There are cases where people will be extorted or blackmailed. There is the stereotype of debtors getting beat-up or thrown into the river if they don't pay up. The anti-gambling establishment will point to bankruptcy and corruption as reasons to stamp out illegal gambling. Politically it can't hurt the cops, D.A., etc. to bust a gambling ring prior to an election. It won't be beneath the cops to bust even the smallest of small time players. These are the easiest people for the cops to get, which will lead them to bigger fish to fry.

Although society puts a low priority on it, it is best not to sports gamble illegally.

The Refs

2005 was a particularly bad year for the referees, umpires and officials. They tended to make mistakes in big spots, sometimes being suckered by players into making bad calls. This can be very frustrating to the sports gambler. Breaks are part of the game and you can never predict which way they will go.

In the 2006 Super Bowl, I personally picked Seattle +3. *I figured right on this one.* Everyone was favoring the tough Steelers and wasn't giving Seattle much credit. I knew that Seattle was an **underrated underdog** and a good bet. Well, guess what? The refs did their best to take that game away from Seattle making lousy calls at critical times. I lost my money. *"Snap back to reality ohp there* *goes gravity.* " It should be said that Seattle didn't help their own cause by dropping passes and poor play calling, but I think it's safe to say the refs had a hand in keeping Seattle from covering with those extra three points.

You have to wonder sometimes about the refs and umpires. They are supposed to be our best and should not be a factor into the betting equation, but sometimes they do. What's going on here? First of all it's a very difficult job. Action happens super fast and quick decisions are difficult. Sometimes if you're playing a sport, it is easier to *feel* the foul, or you *know* if you were safe or not. But when you're only watching the action, and not actually in the play, it can be difficult to judge. The massive television coverage and instant replay has brought more pressure and scrutiny upon officials. Hometown crowd pressure has to at least have some play in it. Like athletes who make mistakes and errors, the refs and umps do also. It's part of the game and you have to accept it and move on.

Still, the officials could do a better job of it though. Sometimes umps and refs get together to correct a bad call, but not always. Everybody in the park knows the call is wrong but they won't do anything about it. The officials need to update some rules and make better, quicker use of technology to get it right. The umpires in baseball at all levels need to call more consistent strikes and be less pompous. They need to get younger football refs and train, pay and treat them like professionals. It would be wise for any sports gambler to take note of any ump or official that catches your eye negatively. Check if he's working a game that you want to bet. Box scores usually name the officials and you can ask the leagues what crews are working what games. You might want to reconsider that particular bet.

Although I have never heard of a high ranking official being busted for throwing a game recently, it would be naïve to think that there is no possibility of it. The refs are human, too. There is a long list of players, ex-players, coaches and managers who have been involved in some degree in illegal sports gambling. The refs have, at times, been accused of conspiracies to promote better match ups for the TV networks. Of course the leagues and refs deny any bias or wrongdoing. For now I think that we should keep one eye on the refs and hold them more accountable.

Beautiful Women

If I have noticed anything in sports, it's the beautiful women who play and follow sports. There are beautiful women at football games. There are beautiful women at hockey games. There are beautiful women at NASCAR. There are beautiful women everywhere in sports. Some are spectators, some are coaches and players, some are family members, some are there to entertain and cheer. And I know there are beautiful women gambling on sporting events. There has been a much-needed rise in acceptance of women as sports fans over the past 25 years or so; no longer does the stereotype of bimbos and sex objects apply. Women can be powerfully intelligent and objective concerning the world of sports.

It's only going to get better. Look around at the youth sport leagues in America. While young boys have been slipping off to video games and x-treme sports, young girls have been filling up the team sport rosters, many playing in boys' leagues. The sweeping action of **Title IX** in college sports - Title IX which mandated equal spending and attention for women's sports has opened the door of opportunity through sports for women. There are far more female student athletes now than in years past.

While the U.S.A. men's Olympic teams have mostly been disappointing lately, U.S.A. women's teams have been medaling, raising the interest, participation, and involvement of women in sports. This all adds up to more women players, spectators, coaches, sports fans and sport gamblers – even female bookies.

For anyone who is interested, it would seem to me that love and romance can be found on the common ground of sports gambling. Sporting events make for nice dates and what better way to raise the interest than having a stake in the outcome.

Whether gambling or not there is no doubt that all across America, from the youth fields to the pro arenas, beautiful women are all around sports.

BE YOUR OWN BOOKIE

While in no way, shape or form does this book advocate or try to promote any illegal activity, you have to look at all of your options in life. Since most gamblers lose their money to bookies, why not join the more profitable side of sports gambling? If you love sports, have an entrepreneurial spirit, possess a good work ethic, and don't mind a little danger, why not become a bookie? Well, you better think about it. Anytime you're conducting an illegal business, bad things can happen. You can lose friends over unpaid debts. You can get robbed of your profits. You can get busted by the police and get fined or go to jail. You have to weigh all of the risk against the benefits if you want to become a bookie. If you want to become a bookie. . . . . .

If you decide you want to become a bookie, you might as well become the best bookie you can be. There is nothing like being your own boss, and as the bookie, you get to set your own lines and rules.

So how can you get started? Obviously as in any business, the best way to know the business is to work for someone else for a while. If you are currently using a bookie, you might want to ask if he or she needs any help. You might be surprised at the positive response you'll get. Even a limited number of hours will benefit. Clerking, answering the phone, running errands, learning the business from the ground up over time will be the most valuable teacher.

Once you're ready to set out on your own, it would be best to start out small and feel your way along. While it is best to be knowledgeable of all possible sports bets, and you should offer **lines** that your customers would want, perhaps it is best at first to limit what you offer to what you are most familiar with. Over time give your customers some freedom and they will become better and more loyal customers.

Be very clear about your rules, be polite, on time, and professional. Be clear about your hours, about **juice** and **settle-up day**. Be consistent, pay out to winners promptly. Run your business with professionalism and courtesy. You'll get burned once in awhile by a few dead-beats, but you'll more than make up for it with profits. Simply don't let the dead beats play again.

How do you get customers? On a small scale you can start a football **parlay** at your work place. Collect the money as the cards are being turned in and pay out to the few winners and keep the profits. Maybe build your customer base from there. Another way would be to throw a sports party. Throw a Super Bowl party with **action** offered. Or maybe a **March Madness** party. Sometimes a boxing pay-per-view party with simple wagers offered can draw some gambling interest. You can rent a banquet room, supply food and drink. Sometimes a back room of a bar or restaurant is an ideal location. Invite people with money and interest in sports. Friends, co-workers, classmates, girlfriends, your insurance guy. Offer **lines** on what ever sporting events your watching. It wouldn't hurt if someone won big; it's good for the overall future business. These people know other gamblers and soon you will have plenty of business. Some people actually don't mind losing. It's a way for them to flaunt their money. They like to talk about how much money they lost on this team or that. They like to gamble and be a player.

Once you get the business established, be sure to give your customers individual numbers to identify themselves with and for your record keeping. It's harder for the cops to trace any customers that way. Start the I.D. numbers in the hundreds such as 301, 302... It will make your business appear larger and more powerful to your clients. Never reveal how much money you're making or how many clients you actually have.

One thing you don't want to do is mix any other illegal activity such as drugs or prostitution with your sports gambling operation. Don't attract any unnecessary negative attention. Don't drink to excess and do not keep any illegal substances or materials at your place of business.

Where would you set up shop to take bets? It depends on how big your book is. Ideally you want a place where there is regular traffic, such as a deli, bar, or barber shop. Customers could stop by or call at your set hours, placing bets without attracting too much attention.

You could run this business out of a home office. There is a method where you as a bookie can set up an 800# phone answering service. It can be set up in a foreign country such as Canada. You can post your **lines** with that answering service daily or more often, if you like. Your clients can phone in their **wagers** to that 800# after they listen to your **lines**. You can then call the 800# to find out what their **wagers** are. Bookie and client can then meet on **settle-up** day to either collect or pay accordingly. This way, even though the client and bookie both live in the same community . . . technically, the gambling transaction takes place offshore. The gambler/bookie relationship is only indirectly linked. Of course you will have to pay for this service, with the cost depending on how elaborate a system you want.

How your local authorities will view this is anybody's guess, but this is how some established bookies do operate.

If you're going to rent a small office, get one on an upper floor, so that you can sense trouble coming. Try to get one with an inside hallway so that it won't be open for the public to see. Some people have advocated acquiring a false identity. Apparently in some off-beat publications you can send away for false I.D.'s and Social Security numbers. To each his own, but my thinking on this is it would just get you into deeper trouble. One guy I know of drove around in a van while taking bets on a cell phone, between the hours of 10 am and noon. This is rather extreme, but I guess the cops couldn't pin him down.

Football season will be your busiest time of year. Some bookies shut down after the Super Bowl. That's where you can pick-up some extra business. You can offer **lines** on basketball, baseball, hockey, golf, Nascar, and more. There is always room for a good businessman. There is always room for a good bookie. The main points you want to remember that will keep you in good standing are:

- Be professional
- Be courteous
- Be consistent
- Be clear regarding your rules
- Pay out to winners in a timely fashion
- Don't mix other illegal activities with your sports gambling operation.
- Don't be greedy.

WHY *NOT* TO SPORTS GAMBLE

Of all the chapters in this book, this chapter has, by far and away, more material written than any other. There is a downside to anything and sports gambling has its share.

Most anything is okay in **moderation**, but to those who overindulge, sports gambling can lead one down a path of serious negative addiction. There have been scores of studies citing the negative effects of gambling in general. Teenagers and children under the legal gambling age of 18 have been able to gamble through deception. This is becoming a more pervasive problem, which can lead to more serious risk taking such as substance abuse and unprotected sex.

Studies show that 2% of all adults end up addicted to gambling. Some people become pathological gamblers whose relationships, finances, and social status all suffer because of their gambling.

Studies show that some people's brains are wired differently. They have an abnormal craving for stimulation, combined with an out-of-control impulsiveness. They are never satisfied even when winning, and will continue to gamble at all cost.

There are plenty of highly critical anti-gambling organizations who claim that gambling corrupts local and state governments, guts local economies, and preys upon the weak and poor. Gambling has led some to divorce and despair causing bankruptcies and even murder and suicide.

As far as sports gambling is concerned, there is always the possibility of corrupting the athletes, umpires and other officials. While a professional athlete who is well paid would have a lot to lose *(just ask Pete Rose)* making the pros less vulnerable, the student athlete is much more vulnerable and you have to wonder about the officials sometimes. There are studies that show college athletes have bet with **bookmakers** with significant amounts of money on the line. More than 5% of male athletes in one survey admitted to betting on a game in which they participated. They have admitted providing information for gambling purposes and some even took money to try to **fix** games by playing poorly. This has been documented and people have gone to jail. Obviously this is not good and shouldn't be tolerated.

Obviously one big reason not to *illegally* sports gamble is the threat of going to jail, or at the very least, getting arrested and having to pay lawyers and court costs.

I know of a young middleclass girl who bet modestly through a bookie, mostly on football. Well guess what. In the bigger investigation to crack the bookies' gambling ring, they tapped her phone lines, questioned her life style and arrested her when she bet on behalf of other people over the phone line. She never went to jail but still was made to feel like a criminal and cost her money.

Anytime you use the internet to sports gamble, as a lot of people do, you must use caution and good judgment. Cyber criminals are becoming more bold and have been attacking gambling websites. Usually, it is more of a problem for the sportsbook, but there is always the risk of identity theft and flat out fraud. Blackmail is sometimes used by cyber criminals as is extortion. It would be wise if you're going to gamble online to use money orders or Western Union and minimize what the internet knows about you.

Life is full of risk and dangers and sports gambling is not good for some people. But then again, eating too many donuts is not good for some people either. There are only so many ways to tell you to use moderation and good judgment. If you think you're having problems and need some help, here are some organizations which may help you.

National Coalition Against legalized Gambling
www.ncalg.org

Look for Gamblers Anonymous in your local phonebook

www.istoppedgambling.com

1-888-lastbet

www.gam.anon.org

GLOSSARY - TERMS AND DEFINITIONS

Parlay?

Point Spread?

Over-Under?

Juice?

Teaser?

Push?

FAVORED?

Giving Odds?

TERMS AND DEFINITIONS

To better understand sports gambling you must first become familiar with all the terms and definitions. You must become familiar with all the different types of bets. Without this knowledge, or even if you only have limited knowledge, you and your money will soon be parted. Try to understand as much as you can. This knowledge is essential to your successful and happy experience as a sports gambler.

In the text of this book, these terms will sometimes be **highlighted** so that you can refer to this chapter if you like.

Action – a bet or wager of any sort.

Action Bet – Action Ticket – The house has the right to change the odds or drop a game altogether. Sometimes in baseball the listed starting pitchers don't start for some reason. If this occurs, then all bets are null and void. It's part of the fine print.

Bet – Any risk of money or other valuable property, based on the outcome of a sporting event.

Betting Line – Odds or point spread on a particular sporting event.

Beard – A person who places bets on behalf of someone else, shielding the bettor's true identity.

Board – a scoreboard displaying all the contests that you can bet on, at what odds or point spreads, what the house or bookies have available for you to bet on.

Bookie – A person who runs a gambling operation and takes bets, takes in bets, collects money, and pays out to winners while taking out a commission for him/herself.

Bookmaker – Also known as a bookie, a bookmaker can be more sophisticated, more professional, also taking bets collecting money, paying out to winners and charging a commission.

Buying Points – A bettor can choose to add or subtract a point from the betting line. The cost is in extra juice. If the bettor wins, he wins less than normal, if he loses, he loses more than normal. Exactly how much is negotiable.

Canadian Line – a combination money line and goal line in hockey.

Example: Tampa Bay Lightning at DetroitRedwings

-1-1/2 +130   +1-1/2 -150

If bettor bets $100 on Tampa Bay and they win by two or more goals, bettor wins $130. If they lose or only win by one goal, then bettor loses $100.

If bettor bets $150 on Detroit and they win or lose by only one goal, then bettor wins $100. If Detroit loses by more than one goal, then bettor loses $150.

Casino – A building or establishment which promotes the business of gambling.

Circled Game – A game in which the house limits the amount which can be bet. Usually due to unusual circumstances.

Cover – To beat the point spread. Example: Washington favored by six wins by seven thus covering the spread; or Washington was a three point underdog losing by only one, thus covering the spread.

Credit – Entrusting payment of a debt. Accounting entry of payment.

Creditor – Someone who is owed money for a debt.

Debtor – Someone who owes money for a debt.

Dimeline – A 10 point difference on a money line between a favorite and an underdog.

Dumbmoney – Small bets by yahoos who know nothing about gambling.

Edge – A margin of advantage.

Exotics – Unusual bets like which player will score first or which team will win the coin toss; how many yards will a certain running back get.

Favored – When a team or individual is considered stronger and more likely to win over the underdog.

Favorite – The one team or individual who is considered stronger and most likely to win over the rest.

Fix – To try to influence or control the outcome of a contest by unfair or illegal means.

Future Bet – Betting on how well a team will do or who will win the championship before the season has started.

> *Example: The odds are 15-1 that the **Marlins** will win the 2008 World Series. Bet $1000 on the Marlins and if they win, you collect $15,000.*
>
> *The over-under for the **Ravens** is nine wins. If you bet $1,000 on the over and the Ravens win 10 or more games, you would collect a little more than $1,900.*

Giving Odds – Betting a larger amount to win a smaller amount.

Handle – The sum of both sides of a bet.

Handicapper – A person who analyzes games and events and sets the odds or betting lines for gambling purposes.

Hedging – Betting both sides of a bet so as to limit any potential losses.

Hook – ½ a point in a point spread.

Example: Cleveland -3-1/2 or Cleveland minus three and a hook.

House – The casino, internet, sportsbook, or bookie or agent who is taking bets.

House Edge – The built in advantages such as juice and long odds the house enjoys against the bettor.

Juice – The cut or commission, usually 10% that the house or bookie takes for setting up and running the gambling operation.

Laying Odds – Taking the favorite and risking a larger amount of money to win less.

Limit – The top amount of money the house or bookie will allow you to bet on each particular contest.

Line – It's sports gambling's method of evening up a contest by handicapping one team or the other with points or odds, thereby attracting bets evenly on both teams.

Line Movement – The numbers may change over a few days if too many people are taking one side of a bet. The house wants equal action on both sides of a bet, and will move the line to attract betting on weak side to even up the action.

Line Shopping – Seeking out the differences in all the betting lines that are available to you.

March Madness – College basketball's playoff tournament to determine a national champion. Occurs in March through early April after the regular season.

Middled – If the score of a contest falls between two possible bets, such as when the opening line is Steelers +3 and the line moves to Steelers +5. Then the Dolphins win by four (24-20). Then people who bet Dolphins -3 and people who bet Steelers +5 would both win.

Moderation – Avoiding extremes and limiting one's indulgence to keep within reasonable limits.

Money Line – Odds of one team either winning or losing with no point spread involved. This penalizes the favorite by risking more to win less.

> *Example: Cubs -140 at Mets +130. If you take the Cubs, you risk $140 to try to win $100. If you take the Mets, you risk $100 to try to win $130.*

N.C.A.A. – National Collegiate Athletic Association.

Nevada – State in which most legal gambling takes place at one of the many casinos.

Newspaper Line – The point spreads or money lines that appear in the most common newspapers. Sometimes they are wrong or misleading from the lines that you can actually bet.

Odds – The difference that one team is favored over another. How likely is the outcome.

Odds Maker – A person who sets the point spread or money line by analyzing tons of information.

Off – This particular contest is no longer being bet on. The action is taken off the board.

Offshore Sportsbook – A gaming business or operation that is located outside of the United States such as a Caribbean Island. Sports gaming can bet here by the internet or 800 phone number.

Open – The very first odds or line that is posted subject to change.

Oregon – State which sells pro-football parlay tickets.

Overrated – A team or individual who is judged by some or most of the general public as being better than they actually are.

Over-Under – Betting on the total number of points scored by both teams will be either over or under a certain number.

Example: You can either bet over or under 45 in the Colts-Jets game.

Actual score:	*Colts 28*
	Jets 20
Over Wins	*Total 48*

Or there are future over-unders

*Example: The **Reds** will win 82 games this year. If you think the Reds will win more, bet over. If you think the Reds will win less, bet under.*

Paper Trading – Mock betting, keeping track of imaginary bets on real games. Seeing how much you would win or lose without betting real money.

Parlay – A bet which involves two or more games or events in combination. All games or events must be won in order to win bet. The pay-off is higher than if games were bet separately, but you must win all. If one game is a tie, then the winnings are reduced.

> *Example:*   *Bears -3 vs. Eagles*
>
>   *Lions   +4 vs. Raiders*
>
>   *Packers - 4 vs. Falcons*

This is a three game parlay. If you win all three, then you win a big payout. If you win two games and lose one, then you lose the entire bet.

Pick or Pick-Em – Teams are judged equal and you get to pick either without any points handicapping either side. Just pick who you think is going to win.

Point Spread – Also known as the line or the spread. It is the number of points that a favorite is handicapped or the number of points an underdog is given to even up a contest for betting purposes.

Prognosticator – A person who analyzes and predicts how teams will do before the season starts, usually employed by the media.

Propositions – Exotic bets such as who will win the coin toss or how many home runs will be hit in a given game.

Puck Line – Slang for hockey betting – sometimes it's a straight goal differential, sometimes it's goal and money line combined.

Pundant – A person who has an educated opinion on a game or sporting event. One who predicts and speculates.

Push – A tie where neither gambler or house wins. All money is returned.

Example: Ram +4 vs. Bengals

Bengals win 20 – 16, thus it's a tie as far as sports gambling is concerned.

Reverse – A high risk bet where a gambler can either win up or lose down up to ten times their bet.

> *Example: If you take Dallas +3 for $1,000 and Dallas wins by 4, that is a $1,000 winner. If you take Dallas +3 for $1,000 and Dallas loses by 10, that is a $7,000 loser.*

Road Dog – When an underdog is playing on the road at the favorite's home field or court.

Settle Up Day – A day designed by the gambler and bookie when money changes hands to settle the account based on previous wagers.

Side – To take one side of the bet, either the favorite or the underdog – one side or the other.

Smart Money – Money bet by pros who bet objectively and with knowledge.

Sports Bar – A business establishment that caters to sports fans. It televises sporting events where many people gather to eat, drink, socialize and be sports fans.

Sportbook – A gambling business or operation that makes its living on accepting bets on sporting events.

Sports Radio – Radio talk shows devoted to sports. Many different stations all dispensing scores and information, featuring players, coaches, sports writers.

Square – A not-so-smart yahoo who gambles foolishly.

State Commissions – A legal check and balance system that individual states set up to police, manage, and govern over that state's legal gambling establishment.

Super Bowl Board – A one hundred square board in which gamblers can purchase as many squares as they want. Each square is assigned two numbers, one each from the two teams that are competing. If the score of the game ends on those two numbers, then you win the whole pot. The catch is you can't pick your numbers. They are randomly determined after the board is filled up. Some boards divide the winners by halves or quarters.

Taking Odds – Betting on the underdog or betting on smaller amount to win a larger amount.

Example: 8 to 5 money line

Bet $5 to win $8 or $7 with juice

Teaser – A bet where the bookmaker teases the gambler with extra points above or below the normal betting line. The catch is the gambler has to bet two or more games parlay style to win bet. Lose any game and you lose entire bet. Plus, more juice is taken out of winners.

Example: Normal Line Dallas -6 vs. Washington

Teaser	*Dallas even vs. Washington*
Or	*Dallas -12 vs. Washington*

Bet in combination with:

Normal line	*Chicago -4 vs. Minnesota*
Teaser	*Chicago even vs. Minnesota*
Or	*Chicago -8 vs. Minnesota*

Must win both games no matter what lines you pick.

Throw A Game – When a player or coach tries to lose a game by playing poorly. The coach or player would rather lose the game and win the bet by influencing the outcome for gambling purposes.

Totals – Total points or goals scored by both teams combined.

Tout – A person who claims to have knowledge to predict the outcome of a game or sporting event.

Tout Service – A business who, for a price, will sell you their knowledge and predictions.

Under – When a total score of both teams falls under a specified number or total wins falls under a specified number.

Example:　　　*Twins 9*　　　*Tigers 5*

Over – under is 16　　*Under wins*

Or

Over-under before season begins for the Mets is 90.

Mets go on to win 86 games　　　*Under wins*

Underdog – The team or individual who is judged weaker and less likely to win. The underdog is given points or odds to even up the contest for gambling purposes.

Underrated – A team or individual who is judged by some or most of the general public as not being as good as they actually are.

Vigorish – The cut or commission the house or bookie takes out of the money that is wagered. It is their commission for setting up and operating the gambling operation – also known as the juice.

Wager – A bet or something gambled.

Wise Guy – A smart professional sports gambler who bets intelligently.